Contents

People in the story

Nat Marley: a New York private investigator
Jorge Hernandez: Nat Marley's client
Stella Delgado: Nat Marley's personal assistant
Mike Lopez: an old friend of Jorge Hernandez
Joe Blaney: a friend of Nat Marley, ex-NYPD (New York Police Department)
Captain Oldenberg: a police officer with the NYPD

Cambridge English Readers

Level 1

Series editor: Philip Prowse

Ten Long Years

Alan Battersby

CAMBRIDGE

CAMBRIDGE
UNIVERSITY PRESS

University Printing House, Cambridge CB2 8BS, United Kingdom

Cambridge University Press is part of the University of Cambridge.

It furthers the University's mission by disseminating knowledge in the pursuit of education, learning and research at the highest international levels of excellence.

www.cambridge.org
Information on this title: www.cambridge.org/9781107621787

First published 2013
Reprinted 2013

Printed in the United Kingdom by Hobbs the Printers Ltd

Typeset by Aptara Inc.
Map artwork by Malcolm Barnes
Illustrations by Nick Hardcastle

A catalogue record of this book is available from the British Library.

ISBN 978-1-107-621787 paperback
ISBN 978-1-107-656017 paperback plus audio CD

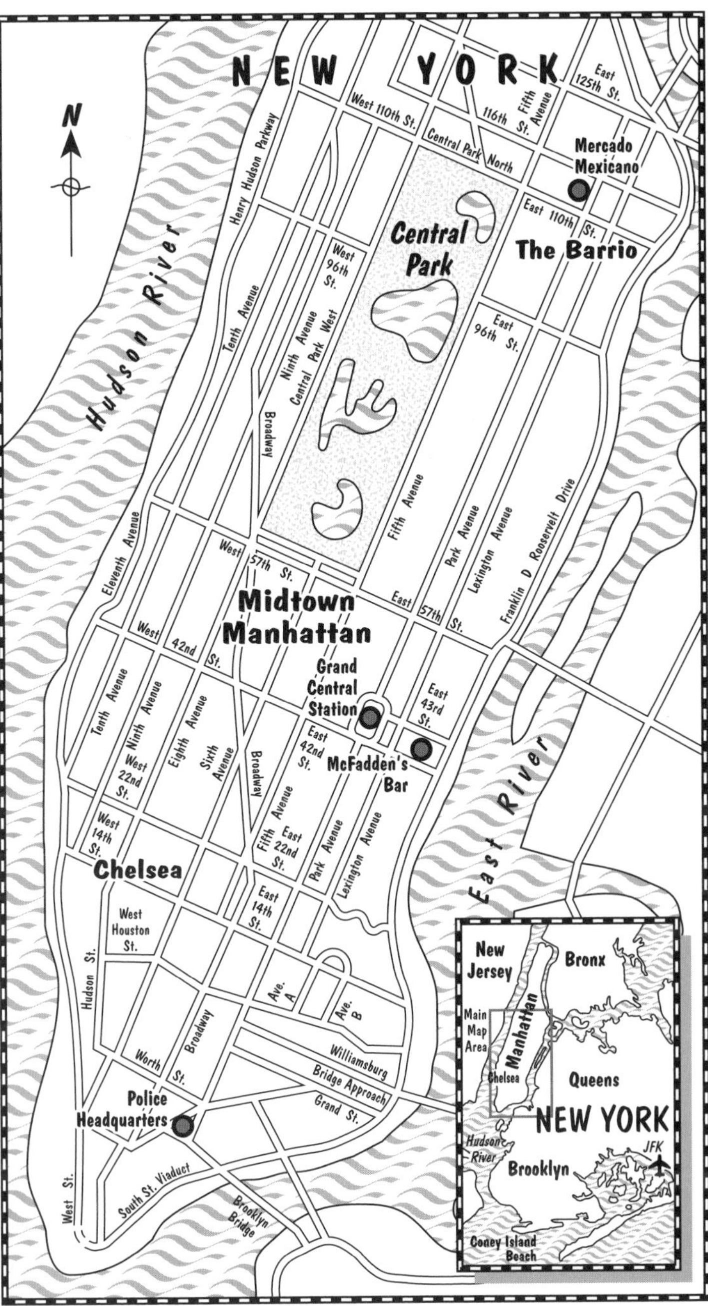

NEW YORK
N
Hudson River
Henry Hudson Parkway
West 110th St.
116th St.
Fifth Avenue
East 125th St.
Central Park North
Mercado Mexicano
East 110th St.
Central Park
The Barrio
West 96th St.
Tenth Avenue
Ninth Avenue
Central Park West
East 96th St.
Broadway
Fifth Avenue
Park Avenue
Lexington Avenue
Franklin D Roosevelt Drive
Eleventh Avenue
West 57th St.
East 57th St.
Midtown Manhattan
West 42nd St.
Grand Central Station
East 43rd St.
Tenth Avenue
Ninth Avenue
Eighth Avenue
Sixth Avenue
Broadway
East 42nd St.
McFadden's Bar
West 22nd St.
Fifth Avenue
East 22nd St.
Park Avenue
Lexington Avenue
East River
West 14th St.
Chelsea
East 14th St.
West Houston St.
Hudson St.
Ave. A
Ave. B
Broadway
Worth St.
Williamsburg Bridge Approach
Grand St.
Police Headquarters
West St.
South St. Viaduct
Brooklyn Bridge
New Jersey
Bronx
Main Map Area
Manhattan
Chelsea
Queens
NEW YORK
Hudson River
JFK
Brooklyn
Coney Island Beach

Chapter 1 *McFadden's Bar*

One April evening, I went for a beer after work in McFadden's Bar on Second Avenue. A lot of people were in there, but I found a table. I sat down with my drink and started to read the *Daily News*.

The name's Nat Marley and I'm a New York private investigator. Before that, I was a cop – an NYPD police officer. That's why I know the streets of this city well – which is a great help in my job. People can't always get what they need from the police. Sometimes a wife wants to know if her husband is seeing another woman. Or a parent wants to find their teenage son. That's when they ask for my help.

A guy walked over to my table and asked, "Can I sit here?"

"Of course," I replied.

He had dark hair and a friendly face. His jacket and jeans looked old. He was about thirty-five years old, I thought. In his hand there was a big glass of beer. He put it on the table and smiled at it. Then he turned to me and said, "Doesn't that look beautiful after ten years without a beer?"

He drank fast, closed his eyes and smiled again. "I can't tell you how good that was!" he said.

I put my newspaper down and asked, "Can I get you another drink? You're a thirsty guy."

"That's real kind of you," he replied.

I bought him a beer. This time he drank slowly.

"You didn't have a beer for ten years. Where were you? Saudi Arabia?" I asked.

He waited a minute before speaking. "Someplace where you have a lot of time to think," he replied. "Someplace where you don't want to be. A cold, gray world. A world where you can shout, but no one hears. You can talk, but no one listens."

I understood, but I didn't want to ask any questions just then.

"It feels good to be back in the city again," he went on. "There's no city like New York. But what do you do, mister?"

"The name's Nat Marley," I said. "I'm a private investigator." I gave him my card.

"That's an interesting job," he said. "You must meet all kinds of people." Then he stood up and said, "I'm sorry, I need to go. It's the beer. My head feels kind of funny."

After he went, I thought, "Am I going to see him again?"

Chapter 2 *Old face, new client*

The next morning, I took the number seven train from Queens into Grand Central Station. There I bought two coffees and walked over to my office on East 43rd Street. My personal assistant, Stella Delgado, was at work at her computer. She's a smart, good-looking Puerto Rican who knows a lot about computers. That's a big help in my kind of work.

"Morning, Stella," I said. "I got you coffee."

"Thanks, Nat," she said. "Oh, and you got a client. He's waiting in your office. His name's Jorge Hernandez."

I walked into my office and said, "Good morning, Mr. Hernandez." Then I stopped. I knew his face from McFadden's Bar. "We meet again! Are you feeling all right now?" I asked.

"I'm OK," he said.

"What can I do for you?" I asked.

"I need to find an old friend," he replied. "He was like a brother to me. I tried to find him yesterday, but things change fast in this city. The street where he lived isn't there now. I didn't find anyone I knew. The old neighborhood is gone, but I must find him. It's important."

"Now, I don't like saying this," I said. "But my kind of work isn't cheap. I always ask for one thousand dollars when I start a job."

"A thousand!" he replied. "That's not going to be easy. I can't get that much money quickly."

I looked at him and thought, "This guy needs help and I need new clients. Why not make it easy for him?"

"OK. Can we say half the money now and half when I finish the job?" I asked. "And I'm going to need your friend's name and the name of the street where he lived. Bring me any old addresses you have for him."

After Hernandez left I thought for a second time, "Am I going to see you again?"

* * *

But the next morning, Hernandez was back. He opened his wallet and took out some money.

"There you are, Mr. Marley," he said. "And here's his name and old addresses. Also his street name – the name that people called him on the streets," he said, giving me a piece of paper."

"Thank you, Mr. Hernandez," I said. "We start work now."

I read the paper: Mike 'Mula' Lopez. "Mula? That's the big animal like a horse?"

"Yeah, that's why he got the name. He's a big, tall guy, but he never looked pretty."

"Can you tell me something more?" I asked. "What kind of work did he do?"

"Oh, a little buying and selling on the streets," Hernandez answered, but said nothing more.

"What kind of buying and selling?" I thought, but didn't say. "How old is he now?" I asked.

"About thirty-five," he replied.

I read the addresses. They were all in the Barrio, on the Upper East Side of the city. I knew those streets when I was an NYPD cop. It was a bad neighborhood. Did Hernandez sell drugs on the streets? And was he in jail for ten years?

"Mr. Hernandez, I don't think you're telling me everything," I said. "I don't like working in the dark. You can choose. Take your money and leave. Or you talk and tell me all you know about Lopez."

Chapter 3 *The Barrio, Upper East Side*

Hernandez looked me in the eye. "OK. You need to know," he said. "I wasn't a good guy. I sold drugs on the streets – crack and heroin. Mike Lopez and two friends, Pablo 'Tacos' Rodriguez and Ramon 'Gordo' Garcia worked for me. I was their boss and we made good money. But then I went to jail for ten years. I lost everything. I came out of Sing Sing last week."

"Why do you need to find Lopez?" I asked.

"I got a letter from him when I was in Sing Sing," Hernandez replied. "Lopez wrote: 'I never forget an old friend. When you get out, you're going to be OK. Find me – I got your money.' You see, the cops never found all my money. Lopez had fifty thousand of it. Of course, I never talked to the cops about him. Brothers from the Barrio don't do that. But when I went to the address on the letter, there was nobody there. It was just an old store."

"OK, you want me to find Lopez. Then you can get your drug money?" I asked.

"I know it's wrong," said Hernandez. "But how can I make a new start? In jail, I worked in the kitchens and learned how to cook. Now I want to open a little fast food restaurant."

"I can find Lopez for you," I said. "But my job isn't to get that money."

* * *

Mike Lopez wasn't an easy guy to find. There were many people with the name Lopez in the phone book. Stella made lots of phone calls, but didn't find him. After an hour's work we didn't think he was dead or in jail.

"We need to go to the Barrio to find him," I told Stella. "We have his street name, 'Mula,' and we can ask people about him. I'm going to need your help with Spanish."

"All right," said Stella. "People tell you more when you use their language."

Spanish is the second language of New York City. In neighborhoods like the Barrio, it's the language you hear everywhere on the streets.

We left the office and walked across to 42nd Street, to Grand Central Station. From there we took a number six train to 110th Street. I like using the New York subway. It's quick and cheap – not like New York's cabs.

In the Barrio, we spoke to people in stores and fast food restaurants on Lexington Avenue. After a number of conversations on the street, Stella had something.

"Nat, I just talked to this guy," she began. "He said, 'Try the Mercado Mexicano.' It's a food store on Park Avenue."

We walked across to Park Avenue where we found the store. In the window there were foods from Mexico and Spain. In the store I asked to speak with Mr. Lopez. A woman said, "Señor Lopez isn't here." Stella spoke to her in Spanish. Then the woman went into a room at the back of the store. After two minutes, a big guy came out. He looked friendly.

"How can I help?" he asked.

"I just want to ask some questions," I said. "It's OK, I'm not from the police. The name's Marley and I'm a private investigator. You are Mike Lopez?" I asked.

“That’s me,” he answered.

“And did you use the street name ‘Mula’? I asked.

He gave me a cold look. “People don’t call me that no more,” he said. “Now I got work to do.”

“Wait a minute,” I replied. “An old friend, Jorge Hernandez, is trying to find you.”

“I don’t know the guy,” he said, a little too quickly. “Excuse me, mister. Like I told you, I got work to do.”

Chapter 4 *Old friends, good friends?*

When we got back to East 43rd Street, I called Hernandez on his cell phone. "We found Mike Lopez," I said. "He has a food store in the Barrio."

"That's good," he replied. "What's the address?"

"Wait, Mr. Hernandez. I want to speak with you first, in my office. Is that OK?" I asked.

"All right," he said slowly. "See you in half an hour."

I put the phone down and spoke to Stella: "A job for you. These are the names of two more friends of Hernandez. See what you can find on Rodriguez and Garcia."

Next I made a call to an old friend, Joe Blaney. When I was an NYPD officer, I sometimes worked with Joe. He taught me a lot – all the important things that they didn't teach you at Police Academy. He doesn't work for the police now, but does jobs for me from time to time.

"Joe, I need you to drive a client and me to the Barrio," I said. "And bring your gun. Can you get here in about an hour?"

Then Stella said, "I got something, Nat. And it doesn't look good. It's an old news story from the *Daily News* website."

I read it – Garcia and Rodriguez were both dead. The police found them on the streets of the Barrio. They didn't have guns. But someone shot the two men in the back. And this was about six months after Hernandez went to jail.

TWO DEAD IN BARRIO STREET SHOOTING

When Hernandez got to the office, I asked him to sit down and listen. "I don't think Lopez wants to meet with you," I said. "I'm taking a friend with us to help. I want nothing to go wrong. Don't forget that you asked me to find Lopez. My job is not to find your money."

I gave Hernandez the news story. "Read this," I said. "I'm sorry – it's bad news."

"I knew Pablo and Ramon when I was a kid," he said sadly.

"Now, here's something for you to think about," I said. "There were four friends who worked on the streets of the Barrio. They made good money. But one went to jail. Two died on those streets. And one is doing all right. Why?"

"I don't know," he replied.

"Well, think about it," I said.

Five minutes later Joe got to the office. I told him everything he needed to know about Hernandez. Joe listened, then asked him, "Why did you go to jail?"

"The police found five hundred grams of our heroin in my apartment," he answered. "But I didn't talk to the cops about Lopez, Garcia and Rodriguez. I went to jail and left them to go on selling on the streets."

"Next question," said Joe. "How did the heroin get there?"

"I don't know. I guess I forgot about it," said Hernandez.

"No, I don't think you did," I said. "People who buy and sell drugs don't just forget half a kilo. I guess your friend Lopez put it there and then called the police. I think he wanted to be the boss."

Hernandez looked down at his feet and said nothing.

Chapter 5 *Changes*

Joe drove Hernandez and me to the Barrio and we stopped on Park Avenue, across the street from the Mercado Mexicano. First I wanted to watch the store. We saw a lot of people going in, then leaving with bags of food. Some big expensive cars stopped in front of the store, but only for a short time. People from the cars went into the store and quickly came out, but not with bags. I took photographs of everyone.

After an hour I asked Joe, "What's going on over there?"

"I don't think everybody's buying food," replied Joe.

There was nobody shopping in the store when Joe, Hernandez and I went in. Inside the door I said to Hernandez, "You wait here. I'm going to ask to speak with Lopez first."

Lopez came out of the back door, but now he didn't look friendly. "You're back, Marley. What do you want from me?" he asked.

"I've brought the old friend I told you about this morning, Mr. Lopez. Mr. Hernandez just wants to speak with you."

"Mike, it's good to see you again," said Hernandez, walking up to him. "I did my time in Sing Sing, but I never talked to the cops about you. Nothing. Do you have my money? I need it to make a new start. You see, now I got nothing."

Lopez laughed at him and took five hundred dollars from his wallet. "You're not the boss man now, Hernandez. You're nobody," he said coldly. "Take the money and run. I don't want to see your face in the Barrio again."

Hernandez looked at the money, then looked back at Lopez. "Five hundred dollars! You had fifty thousand of my money!"

Lopez laughed again and said, "Things change in this city. There ain't nothing here for you."

"Oh yeah?" replied Hernandez angrily. "I guess the police need to ask you some questions. Like what are you selling here? And who shot Rodriguez and Garcia?"

"You're a dead man, Hernandez!" shouted Lopez. I saw him quickly put his hand inside his jacket.

But Joe was fast too. Now his gun was in his hands.

"Think again!" he shouted. "Just do what I say. Put your hands behind your head. Turn to the wall, real slow. Now get on your knees." Lopez did what Joe told him.

"We're leaving," I said to Lopez. "Have a nice day!"

When we were back in the car, I said to Joe, "Thanks for your help there. Can you get us back to the office fast?" Then I turned to Hernandez. "Lopez is an interesting friend. But we aren't finished with him."

* * *

Back in my office Hernandez asked, "What am I going to do, Mr. Marley? I don't have much money, I don't have a job, and I can't pay the hotel after this week. I can't live on the streets. Lopez took all my money and now he's rich. And now I feel stupid!"

"You said you wanted to change. It isn't going to be easy, but this is how you do it," I began. "Make Lopez do his time in jail. I know Captain Oldenberg of the NYPD. I worked with him sometimes when I was an NYPD officer. You can make him a very happy cop. Tell him what he needs to put Lopez in jail."

"But it feels wrong – a guy like me talking to the cops," said Hernandez.

"Yes, but look what your old friend Lopez did to you," I said.

Hernandez thought for a time. "All right," he said slowly. "I don't like it, but it's something I must do. But not today. What about in your office tomorrow morning?"

I called Oldenberg.

"Nat Marley speaking. I got something important for you."

"Important, you say!" Oldenberg shouted back at me. I took the phone away from my ear. "I got a lot of work to do, Marley. You got two minutes."

But when I began to tell him Hernandez's story, he stopped shouting and listened. After ten minutes, Oldenberg said, "I can come to your office at ten o'clock tomorrow morning."

Now I felt tired and hungry. "What do you say to steak and fries in McFadden's?" I asked Hernandez.

"You know what the answer's going to be," he replied.

I told Stella: "Time to stop work. Get your coat on. I'm buying dinner."

Chapter 6 *Life after Sing Sing?*

After finishing his steak and fries, Hernandez looked happy. He smiled at us across the table. "I feel good," he said. "Little things in life are important, like enjoying dinner with friends. Sing Sing helped me understand that."

"I know what you're saying," I replied.

"When I first went to jail, I felt like an angry animal," he said. "I hated everybody and everything. I had too much time to think about money. The money that my good friend Lopez had." He laughed and went on: "Now look at me. I'm just thinking about how to buy my next meal."

"I can help you there," said Stella. "My brother José works in a fast food restaurant on Coney Island," said Stella. "He told me they need a new cook."

"Well, I wanted to do something more than that," said Hernandez. "But I can cook. You know I worked in the kitchens in jail. And I guess it's a start."

"OK. I'm going to call José and ask him to speak with his boss," said Stella. She got out her cell phone.

"Were things all bad in Sing Sing?" I asked Hernandez.

"A lot of the time, yes," said Hernandez. "Week after week, nothing changes. You see the same faces and hear the same sounds. There are people that you don't choose to be with. But how do you get away from them? You can't. You feel afraid, but there's nothing you can do. The next day, it's the same – again and again."

"I like the way you talk about things," I said to Hernandez. "I feel like I'm there with you."

"Oh yeah?" said Hernandez, giving me a funny look. "Someone in Sing Sing said that to me too. I took a writing class in jail. The teacher, Louise Armitage, told me: 'Email me when you get out. We can talk more about your writing.'" He took some papers from his jacket. "Well, Mrs Armitage, I tried to do some writing, but it's no good." Then he tore up the papers.

"I'm just Jorge Hernandez from the Barrio. Guys like me don't write. I can only do what I know. Cook burgers and fries and forget what I was. Forget I had money. See you tomorrow, Mr. Marley."

After Hernandez left, I found his papers. "Stella, there's something I need to do at the office," I said. "But you go home now. See you in the morning." When I got to East 43rd Street, I stopped and looked behind me. "Is somebody watching me? Is there somebody standing in that door?" I thought. But I was wrong. Nobody was there.

Back in the office I read some of Hernandez's writing.

The Noises of Sing Sing

When you live and work in the city, you hear noise everywhere you go. Conversations in the streets, cars, subway trains, and music from store fronts. When you get home, you just close the door, say goodbye to noise, and enjoy silence.

In jail, you never find silence. Noise is always there. At any time, day or night, somebody is shouting. Doors open and close. Sleep doesn't come easily because you can't close your ears to noise. You can only think about something you can never enjoy - the beautiful sound of silence.

I thought, “He knows how to use words.” It didn’t take long to find the website of Hernandez’s teacher on the computer: “Louise Armitage, teacher of creative writing.”

I wrote her an email.

My client, Jorge Hernandez, was a student in your class in Sing Sing. He’s out of jail now and he’s going to get work in a fast food restaurant. He’s an interesting guy, and I think he can do a lot with his writing. Give me a call and we can talk about him.

The streets were dark when I left the office. Somebody shouted, “That’s Marley! Get him!” I heard car doors open and close.

“I wasn’t wrong after all,” I thought when I saw two big guys running across the street.

Chapter 7 *"Ten Long Years"*

The two guys took me over to a car and put me in the back. The car drove away fast and took a left onto Lexington Avenue. I knew the man sitting in the back next to me – it was Lopez. There was a gun in his hand.

"OK, Marley. You want to live? Then take me to Hernandez," said Lopez.

What do you do when you're next to an angry guy with a gun? You think quickly and talk fast. "You got the wrong guy, Lopez," I said. "My work with Hernandez is finished. He just wanted me to find you. Nothing more. I don't know where he is."

"Call him!" shouted Lopez.

I didn't want Lopez to find Hernandez. Again I thought quickly.

"I can't, because I don't have his number," I replied. "He called me from pay phones. Hernandez isn't stupid. He doesn't want people to find him. Like I said, I just did the one job for him. I got my money and said goodbye – end of story. Do what you want to me – I can't tell you any more."

Lopez put the gun down and said, "That's too bad. But I never want to see you in the Barrio again. Understood?" Then he told the driver: "Stop the car. Marley's getting out."

I watched the big car drive away down Lexington Avenue. I felt angry and afraid. I wanted Lopez in jail.

The next day, Captain Oldenberg came to question Hernandez. I gave Oldenberg the photos I took the day before. "These are the people from Lopez's store," I said. "You can see that they don't all have bags. Not all of them are shopping for food."

Then I showed Oldenberg and Hernandez into my office and left them to talk. After an hour, Oldenberg asked me to come in.

"Marley, I want to thank you and Mr. Hernandez," said Oldenberg. "We're going to take a look in the Mercado Mexicano and see what we find. Lopez has a lot of questions to answer."

* * *

The next week I got a phone call from Louise Armitage. "Thanks for your email, Mr. Marley," she said. "You know Jorge Hernandez then?"

"Yes," I replied. "I helped him to find an old friend. But this friend wasn't a good one. Now Hernandez wants to make a new start. He's working in a fast food restaurant, but he wants more."

"That's interesting. I don't often meet guys in Sing Sing who can write well. I love Hernandez's writing. He watches people and listens to how they talk. When he puts it down on paper, the words feel just right. How can I meet with him?" she asked.

"You got a pen? … This is his cell phone number," I said. "He needs some new friends now."

* * *

Three months after that, I met with Hernandez after work in McFadden's Bar.

"I'm getting a lot of help from Louise Armitage," he said. "I feel like I'm a new man. After those ten long years in jail, I'm doing something I want to do. I'm living again. I got a lot to learn, but with Louise's help, I can do it."

"Is Jorge Hernandez from the Barrio going to write a book?" I asked.

He gave me a big happy smile. "I know I can now," he said. "I don't know how long it's going to take. But I'm going to get there."

* * *

Two years after that evening, "Ten Long Years" was in the bookstores. It sold well – thousands in the first week. That book changed Hernandez's life and made him famous.

He stopped cooking burgers and fries on Coney Island. It was the first of many books.

Hernandez gave me his first book and I always smile when I open it. He wrote in it: "To Nat Marley, with all my thanks – the guy who bought me a very important beer."